The

Golden

Resume

Also By Brian Robben

Freedom Mindset

How To College

The Golden Resume

Secrets To Acing Interviews And Winning Job Offers

Brian Robben

ISBN-13: 978-1517407063
ISBN-10: 1517407060

Praise from Readers and Reviewers

"I sent out 7 applications last Thursday night. The next morning I had 2 callbacks before lunch. By Saturday I had 4 interviews set. The first time in my life that I had options when choosing employment. If you want the hiring manager and recruiter excited about your resume, you need this in your arsenal."

- Michael Gonzalez

"It seems as though so many books about creating a resume touch on the exact same things. *The Golden Resume* is different. It dives deeper into creating not just a perfect resume, but also a digital brand and ensures that you display yourself to be the best candidate for any job you apply for."

- Hunter Sneed

"Robben's book provides tools that will make you feel like you're hacking the system. With accessible, approachable, and achievable solutions to the search for a profession, *The Golden Resume* is the product, the result, of what can be achieved if the practices outlined in this book were followed. Use it as a guide, an inspiration, or a manual. Use it to shine a light on the daunting path to employment. Use it, and take your success."

- Alexandria Moore

"There are books by folks who write about how to ace your career, and then there are books by Brian Robben. Refreshing, unique, and creative, Robben takes the job search process to another level, enabling the modern job seeker to rise above the norm and truly get what they want. After all, what is life worth if you're not living it on your terms?"

- Albert Qian

"*The Golden Resume* provides you with a 'No B.S.' approach to constructing a resume that will not only impress recruiters, but will have them begging for you to come in for an interview."

- Euan Swan

"Brian Robben's book will be recommended by me to anyone not only writing their resume, but also those who need direction on finding a passion and making movements towards such work. Robben's book on how to build a resume comes out of hundreds of hours of Robben's journey and now career in helping youth reach higher levels of aptitude. Big ideas which are clearly presented which I believe will help those who are crafting a resume include:

1) Finding a narrative in your story
2) Detailing how your online content is important
3) How your personality and gifts can shine through your pursuit of a career."

- Pearl Glacier

"The best thing about *The Golden Resume* is that it doesn't read like one of those stuffy career advice sessions. It's like talking to a friend over coffee -- that is, if your friend happens to be a resume pro. It is detailed and funny and full of practical, brilliant advice from someone who has made the same mistakes we make and learned exactly what we wish we all knew about resumes."

- Amanda Hancock

"If you want to craft your perfect resume, look no further. Brian is an expert in his craft and has the experience to prove it. If you want to be less busy and more productive in your job search, read this book."

- Tam Pham

"This book is an excellent way for people to not miss a beat when crafting a resume and applying to jobs. Brian gets inside the minds of employers and lays out what they are looking for, step-by-step, on these pages. I recommend this book to everyone!"

- Jenn West

"Brian Robben does a tremendous job of writing in a way that makes me feel like I'm having a conversation with him. At no point was I struggling to read it. Brian has great experience and gives great tips on how to stick out in the job search process. He does a nice job of writing in a way that speaks to all majors and career paths. I'm looking forward to winning job offers with Brian's help. Wish I had known about these tips sooner in my career!"

- Mat Harvey

CONTENTS

Chapter 01

One Resume, Two Fates

Before going home for the night, a recruiter reaches for one more resume from her stack.

This time, your name is at the top of the resume.

Like the countless other resumes she has looked at today, she quickly skims your education, your work experience, and your extracurricular activities. Then her eyes scan one final up and down to confirm she didn't miss anything.

In a matter of seconds, she decides your fate. She will drop your resume in one of two different worlds: the rejection pile to the left, or the golden pile (aka the interview pile) to the right.

If your resume lands in the rejection pile, you'll never know what you missed out on and how different your life could have been.

But, consider if your resume lands in the golden pile. What happens next can change the direction of your career and life forever.

Right around the corner is:

- A job of exciting responsibility and fun challenges.
- A clear way to skip the "paying your dues" phase of work.
- A high starting income to help you pay back your student loans, or begin your journey to wealth.
- A dream internship or job that gives you the opportunity to work with interesting people, make a difference in the world, and feel personally satisfied.

As you can see, the stakes are high for one little piece of paper.

Will your resume land in the rejection pile? Or will your resume land in the interview pile, and then the job-offer pile?

The real question is, do you know how to write the resume that gets a second look? Do you know what makes a resume shine so bright that it becomes truly... golden?

Chapter 02

What To Expect

Your job search can be a stressful process. While you try to handle classes or other responsibilities, the personal pressure to get a job, and more importantly the right job, adds up.

It's also hard when your parents, siblings, and friends start questioning your progress. The people who are supposed to be your support end up only raising your anxiety.

If your job search isn't producing any early fruit, each day this situation gets worse because both the pressure to perform and your self-doubt grow stronger.

You naturally start to question the value of your education, your future, and yourself.

But, I'm here to tell you none of this stress and pressure needs to happen. You can avoid it all through reading and following the strategies in this book.

The Golden Resume gives you insight into the recruiter's mind, answers all your resume questions, and hands out secrets to stand out from the crowd and ace interviews.

This book has been created to give you resume and interview essentials in a concise and applicable format.

Before we get any farther, you might ask, "What exactly is a golden resume?" Good question.

When you have a golden resume: it shines, it stands out, it doesn't come in second or third, and it wins gold.

When you do not have a golden resume: it shows rust, it looks the same as every other one, it gets rejected, and it loses. Nobody remembers it.

Addressing Common Objections

I know you'll have objections about why your situation is different and hopeless so you can't have a golden resume. So, I tackled some of the most common excuses I hear:

- If you feel your GPA is too low for a position, this book will show you how to compensate and turn this around as an advantage.
- If you're convinced your major is stopping you from getting a position in a different field, this book will prove your options aren't limited by your major.
- If you never get responses when you submit your resume, you will find key strategies to stand out and get the recruiter excited to meet you.
- If you struggle in interviews, you will get a detailed plan to master the interview process and make the interviewer want to hire you on the spot.

Regardless of your objections, *The Golden Resume* is made for you and your career success.

Overall, your resume holds an incredible weight in getting internships and job offers. Since your first internship or job has an effect on the rest of your career, writing an excellent, golden resume is even more critical to your future.

I've researched, tested, and fine-tuned what makes a golden resume. As I talk about in the next chapter, I'm so thankful I made my resume a priority, because this single document drove me to an exciting job, lucrative salary, and incredibly fortunate situation that continues to bless me to this day.

Because I've experienced this satisfaction, I want you to also experience the exact same feeling! And I know you can do it. You've already taken the first step with buying this book.

Whether you're handing your resume out to employers at a career event, uploading the document online, or emailing your resume, you want it to pack a powerful punch.

After reading this book, your resume will impress the reader so much so that if they don't hire you, they will be personally upset. Now, that's a strong reaction!

What I share in these pages are the proven strategies that top-performers utilize to dominate their job search. If you follow these resume strategies, I guarantee you'll get more interviews and increase your chances for job offers.

So keep reading, because the earlier you finish, the quicker you can write your golden resume and make strides to getting your dream job.

Chapter 03

How I Can Help

My resume served as the launching point for an incredible job search cycle that ended with unreal options.

For example, multiple times I handed over my resume at my college's career fair, an on-campus recruiting event, or in the company's office and the recruiter's eyes lit up as they said, "Wow, look at that," or, "Tell me more about this leadership position."

They didn't even wait for the interview. They wanted to know more. Then I executed my interview strategy, which we will get to later in the book, and the hiring managers loved me.

This one document empowered me to an incredible measure. Now, I'm confident that if a hiring manager had my resume, I could virtually get any interview.

After my first couple go-arounds, my delivery and impression only improved. Of course, my results expanded, too.

In the end, I used my resume to gain multiple job offers and accept an offer in outside sales with the number one company in their industry.

What's even better is I used my leverage from my resume and interview to negotiate my salary to $10,000 more than the initial figure. Plus, I got handed accounts totaling more than one million dollars in yearly sales—which my manager says is, "A situation unheard of."

Although I accepted my job in December 2014, and started work in June 2015, I still get calls and emails asking me to interview because they saw my resume.

Do you want results like this?

Maybe you have your eye on a big internship or job. Maybe you just want one interview.

And, maybe you don't know where to start with your resume.

Maybe you designed your resume without doing any research and you think one standard resume works for different positions.

Maybe you got help from career services, a friend, or a parent, but aren't confident in their advice.

Maybe you believe you have a good resume, but when you apply for jobs, you don't advance to the interview round.

Or maybe you're getting to the interview round, but you fail to communicate well and don't connect with the interviewer—ultimately getting rejected from the job.

The good news is you are in the right place, because I promise you I can help. The same way I've helped dozens of my friends get jobs.

In the next chapter, you'll read a story about me falling on my face thanks to my initial resume.

I share this story because it's also important that you forget about your past results, since now you're in the job search with a new game plan.

Chapter 04

My Background Story That Inspired This Book

The first week of my freshman year of college, I walked into the career services office without a clue how to write a resume. I didn't bring anything with me: no rough draft resume, no list of previous experiences, and not a word on a single sheet paper.

But, because I knew I needed a resume to apply for internships, I went with the philosophy "if I don't know, ask."

So, after talking to a lady from career services, I started from scratch on a blank Word document.

She walked me through the basics: my name and contact information at the top, college information, work experience, and extracurriculars. Then I saved the file, emailed it to myself, and felt positive about my progress.

A month after writing my resume, I searched for internships for the summer in between my freshman and sophomore year. Being an ambitious son of a gun, I sent my resume to Google, the National Football League, and the White House, and another 50-plus organizations.

Days, weeks, months, and a semester passed by, and I heard nothing. Most places didn't spare me a confirmation email saying, "We received your resume and we will get back to you after reviewing it."

So, I smelled something fishy.

I narrowed my resume as the primary suspect for my lack of results. I reviewed it again and realized it didn't look as good as I initially thought after walking out of the career services office.

Honestly, the resume I sent out was terrible, absolutely awful! I recreated for you what it basically looked like. Check it out.

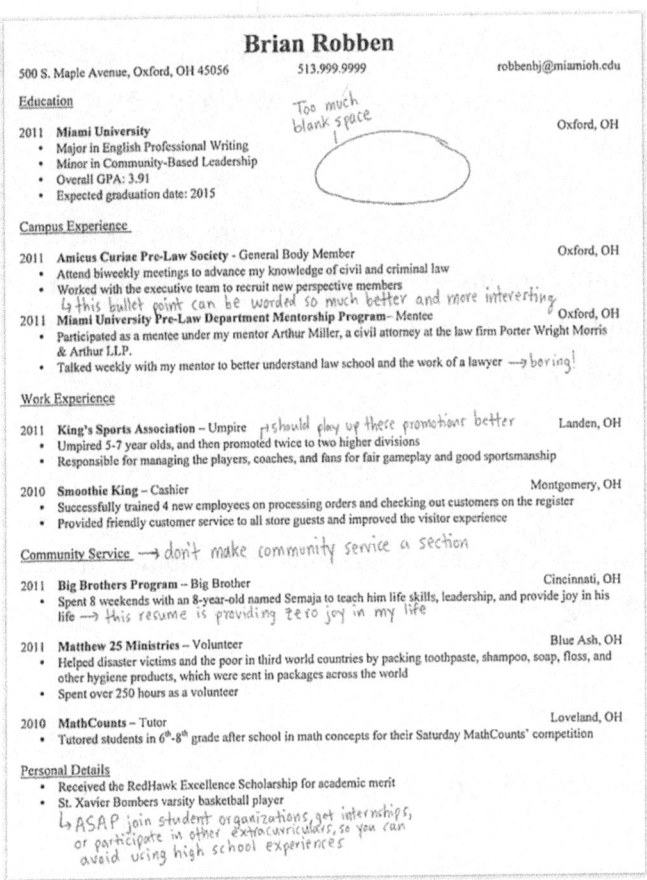

Brian Robben

500 S. Maple Avenue, Oxford, OH 45056   513.999.9999   robbenbj@miamioh.edu

Education

[handwritten: Too much blank space]

2011   **Miami University**   Oxford, OH
- Major in English Professional Writing
- Minor in Community-Based Leadership
- Overall GPA: 3.91
- Expected graduation date: 2015

Campus Experience

2011   **Amicus Curiae Pre-Law Society** - General Body Member   Oxford, OH
- Attend biweekly meetings to advance my knowledge of civil and criminal law
- Worked with the executive team to recruit new perspective members *[handwritten: this bullet point can be worded so much better and more interesting]*

2011   **Miami University Pre-Law Department Mentorship Program**– Mentee   Oxford, OH
- Participated as a mentee under my mentor Arthur Miller, a civil attorney at the law firm Porter Wright Morris & Arthur LLP.
- Talked weekly with my mentor to better understand law school and the work of a lawyer *[handwritten: → boring!]*

Work Experience

2011   **King's Sports Association** – Umpire *[handwritten: should play up these promotions better]*   Landen, OH
- Umpired 5-7 year olds, and then promoted twice to two higher divisions
- Responsible for managing the players, coaches, and fans for fair gameplay and good sportsmanship

2010   **Smoothie King** – Cashier   Montgomery, OH
- Successfully trained 4 new employees on processing orders and checking out customers on the register
- Provided friendly customer service to all store guests and improved the visitor experience

Community Service *[handwritten: → don't make community service a section]*

2011   **Big Brothers Program** – Big Brother   Cincinnati, OH
- Spent 8 weekends with an 8-year-old named Semaja to teach him life skills, leadership, and provide joy in his life *[handwritten: → this resume is providing zero joy in my life]*

2011   **Matthew 25 Ministries** – Volunteer   Blue Ash, OH
- Helped disaster victims and the poor in third world countries by packing toothpaste, shampoo, soap, floss, and other hygiene products, which were sent in packages across the world
- Spent over 250 hours as a volunteer

2010   **MathCounts** – Tutor   Loveland, OH
- Tutored students in 6th-8th grade after school in math concepts for their Saturday MathCounts' competition

Personal Details
- Received the RedHawk Excellence Scholarship for academic merit
- St. Xavier Bombers varsity basketball player

[handwritten: ASAP join student organizations, get internships, or participate in other extracurriculars, so you can avoid using high school experiences]

My freshman year resume has no story or narrative behind it about who I am and what I want. The bullet points are boring, making me appear just like every other applicant. Nothing on this resume makes me stand out. There is wasted space, mixed with wasted words or poor word choices. This resume is so bad!

What I didn't realize my freshman year when I blasted out my resume is that building a golden resume takes time. It takes much more than half an hour of work.

Also, the reality is that many career service offices are understaffed, not specialized, and unfortunately not fit for the great responsibility of influencing one of the most important documents in your life.

Bless their heart though, from my experiences, their underperformance isn't from a lack of effort or lack of kindness. They're presented the task of being general enough to help all students, while facing the impossible challenge of being specialized enough to offer specific advice for each student in different industries. Career services often can't help you as much as you want them to.

Moving back to my story, I got over my upset feelings about failing and became motivated to get the best possible outcome.

I promised myself that I would never again miss out on career opportunities because of something I can control, which in this case is my resume.

Over my college years, I decided to teach myself about what a successful resume looks like through reading books, business articles, and blog posts. Plus I watched videos and listened to experts. I also sought out business mentors and learned from them. Then I combined all this information to solidify my new strategy.

Also, since that day of enlightenment my freshman year, I became the guy who immediately updates his resume after getting back semester grades, taking a new job, or receiving an award. I still do this today. If I don't keep tweaking my resume, it'll lose its golden shine.

Overall, I've spent hundreds of hours on my resume over the years, like Leonardo Da Vinci's precision when stroking a painting. (Well that's what I imagine anyway.) In that time, I've learned so many tricks and ways of marketing myself. And you know what? Other people have noticed.

My sister first asked me to review her resume after she heard how many people struggled at a career fair, while she noticed how many interviews I received. She realized how my success was pretty rare for students. Then, my friends and housemates noticed my success, and asked me what my secrets were.

Soon, multiple people wanted my help. I ask them questions about what position they were going for, and strategically edited their resume.

Through these interactions, I realized that many students have a hard time creating a good resume. Many times they have virtually no clue how to write a resume that really wins them a dream job.

The biggest problem I found is how many students write a general resume without a specific purpose. I couldn't let more students miss the resume mark when their career weighed in the balance, so I decided to write this book.

My purpose is to debunk the resume myths and provide clear, straightforward advice that not many people know. The best part for you is that I designed the book so you won't have to go through the pains of teaching yourself how to write a successful resume through trial and fire, like I did.

Since you're in the right place reading this (and depending what your resume currently looks like), you can also create a masterpiece out of your resume.

Let's keep on moving. There's no better place to start creating a golden resume than first understanding your audience—recruiters and hiring managers.

Chapter 05

Inside The Mind Of Recruiters And Hiring Managers

If you want to develop a purpose for your resume, you've got to better understand the mind of the people evaluating you. What exactly are they thinking? It's your job to figure it out.

On the surface, it's easy to assume a recruiter's job description consists of only finding applicants and doing pre-screen interviews. You might spend time researching the company and their top leaders, but you probably don't think about the lower-level recruiter. But you should.

A big step in developing the golden resume is to understand a recruiter on a deeper level. When you know a recruiter's job responsibilities, worries, needs, and desires, then you can maximize your presentation to them. And then, suddenly, your resume is on the desk of a company president.

Because the company's future results depend on the quality of its employees, recruiters play an important role. They often recruit locally and nationally to build pools of qualified applicants for times of need.

Specifically, if there is an open position, it's the recruiter's job to swiftly use their resources to fill the vacancy. Without much notice, the recruiter also needs to have resources and contacts in place to hire quality applicants if the organization decides it's time to grow.

Beyond their general responsibilities, a recruiter's day-to-day life involves searching for future quality prospects through any means necessary. They mainly utilize the internet, networking, and LinkedIn to recruit.

They screen potential candidates for pictures of questionable behavior and monitor tweets, blog posts, and comments that lack good character. Google search makes it extremely easy to weed out the bad apples.

In a future chapter, I will cover the topic of your online presence and the fact that everything online is an extension of your resume that will be used to judge you. More on that later.

Let's talk about these recruiters. They travel to special events like career fairs for on-campus recruiting. This is where they review resumes and act as the gatekeeper to an applicant's future (or lack of future) with the company.

Since recruiters can be faced with hundreds of resumes (potentially thousands over the year), there isn't enough time to spend minutes reviewing each one. Some studies report that reviewers spend no more than six seconds on average looking at an individual's resume. Six seconds!

That gives you a limited window to make yourself attractive as an applicant.

In the seconds they do spend on your resume, recruiters primarily look at your name, education, most recent work experience, second most recent work experience, and one extracurricular activity.

That is basically it. Although the window is small, there's enough opportunity to make an impact.

Back to the recruiter's perspective. Running through hundreds of resumes is a long task in itself, but the amount is not the most difficult part.

The hardest aspect is deciding who to advance and who to reject, when the resumes all look similar.

Think about it this way. If a recruiter for an accounting firm visits a career fair on a college campus, what kind of resumes are they going to see?

For one, all the resumes will be from the same college. Two: the super majority of resumes will come from accounting majors, who all took similar classes. Three: many applicants will have accounting internships that vary insignificantly. Four: these resumes likely include similar student organizations and clubs.

Recruiters are forced to play a game of Where's Waldo? when no one stands out in the crowd.

In a future chapter, I will show you how to capitalize on everyone else's resume looking the same, so you can take advantage by making your resume unique.

While searching through similar resumes is mundane, many aspects of recruiter's jobs are out of their control, especially when dealing with college students and young professionals.

Recruiters have three main concerns that drive them nuts.

The first factor outside their control is talking with an applicant and only hearing what the applicant thinks they want to hear. Even two or three interviews with the same applicant, depending on the interaction, can leave the recruiter without a good read on him or her.

The recruiter is stuck making a decision where they don't have enough information, because the applicant didn't supply them. But, time is moving, so they make a quick decision to send this person on to the hiring manager or decline them, and hope for the best.

Second, the recruiter will go through an experience where they do get the deeper information they need, and it's all great. From a couple conversations on the phone, double-digit emails back and forth, the recruiter is excited about sending this kid to meet with the hiring manager.

Then the hiring manager loves the applicant as much as the recruiter, and they're convinced it's a perfect fit, so they extend the job offer.

A month later, the once extremely excited applicant declines this offer in lieu of working for another organization. This pains recruiters, because all their effort and time spent with this one person leaves them with nothing to show for it.

In a third pain point for recruiters, the applicant takes the offer, but doesn't contribute well to the team. They misunderstand their boss, don't fit in with the organization's culture, and slow the team down more than help it. This employee eventually gets let go or takes a different job, but the recruiter recognizes this failed situation doesn't look well upon them.

Based on these three examples, do you know what recruiters look for? Check your guesses with these answers.

Recruiters want:

1. Applicants who connect with them in an honest conversation and share what makes them unique.
2. Applicants who give the impression of being loyal and committed to the company for the long haul, meaning they aren't a risk to leave in a couple months.
3. Applicants who can effectively communicate why they are the best candidate for the position through specific explanations.

If a recruiter can check these three items off their list, then they can confidently recommend this applicant to their hiring manager for more interviews and a final decision.

Now that we understand recruiters, it makes it easier for us to connect with them and reach the hiring manager.

☐ Quick tip: Remember, if you're a good applicant, this recruiter essentially needs you as much as you need them. So, not only does a golden resume advance your career, but it's also a helping hand to recruiters.

I told you this document is powerful!

After we analyze why most resumes are ignored, I'll show you step-by-step how to make sure your resume lands in the golden interview pile.

Chapter 06

Why Most Resumes
Are Ignored

Many recruiters have years of experience in reviewing resumes and interviewing.

As we've discussed, one of their biggest pains is finding the right applicant when they all seem the same.

Essentially their job is to find a couple needles in a haystack. The needles are the candidates who are best for the job, and the haystack is the masses of other applicants with similar resumes.

Do you know their favorite cure to help alleviate

this problem? Their easiest solution is to reject applicants who make bad mistakes. This decreases the size of the haystack, and allows them to more easily find the best candidates.

If you avoid the following mistakes, your resume won't get ignored before you're given a chance to interview.

Top Reasons Why Resumes Are Ignored

1. Zero keyword matches.

Through the power of the internet, prescreening services can search for multiple criteria words to narrow down their list quickly.

If your resume is a standard one that you sent out to seven different organizations in some different fields, your odds of meeting the search requirements are extremely low.

2. Not catered to the job description.

If you skip over job descriptions with the thought they're a waste of time and for losers, it's likely you're the one wasting your time applying and losing.

Many times the recruiter writes the job description, so it's simple for him or her to see if you're a fit or not. Humans don't need a search machine to notice a general fact sheet that isn't targeted for their specific position or field.

And certainly don't apply to a position that requires an engineering degree if you don't have one.

3. Only meet qualifications.

If the position requires an engineering major and that's you, then that's a good start. But, if your only claim to the position is your major, and you offer nothing else unique or special, good luck beating all the other applicants.

The difference is huge between barely making the qualifications and being a superior candidate.

4. Questionable internet presence.

If you're applying for a PR, marketing, communications, or a related position, you definitely need some type of internet presence. If you're serious about your field, you will be contributing professional, thoughtful pieces to a site to display your communication skills.

However, every applicant will want some type of credibility from a platform like LinkedIn or Twitter. If a recruiter Google searches your name and can't find you, this brings up concerns about your credibility and trustworthiness.

On the other hand, an internet presence consisting of questionable Tweets, Facebook comments, and pictures where you look like a frat king or queen, will end your application in an instant.

I dive deeper into this topic in the next chapter.

5. The formatting is a mess.

You know when you're about to enter a room, but it's such a mess that you walk right back out? If your formatting is a mess, the reviewer will toss your resume rather than try to make sense of it.

Formatting errors stem from disorganization, overdone bold or italics, unnecessary word dumping, and too much blank space (cue Taylor Swift).

6. Typos are present.

In the resume world, a typo is an unforgivable sin. The recruiter immediately labels you as someone who lacks diligence, attention to detail, and professionalism.

Before they let their mind run down the path of you making a critical error for their company in the future, it's goodbye to you.

7. Numbers are missing in action.

It's a red flag if the only figures on your resume are your grade point average and dates.

Regardless of your major, numbers will always play some role in the position you're applying for and in the world. Obvious jobs where numbers are crucial include investment banking, finance, and statistics.

Yet, numbers matter in marketing, theatre, music, and art, too. Your performance in these roles will depend on how many page views you generate, how many visitors attend the performance, and selling the artwork at the right margin.

8. Overwhelming or underwhelming resume information.

Find the middle point between dumping every semi-related activity you've ever done onto a cramped page, and barely covering three fourths of a resume with your information.

If you're 21 and have to reference an honor society from high school, then you're doing this resume concept wrong. However, if you're 21 and leave off your leadership experience in an organization in college—because you don't think it's relevant— you're also doing it wrong.

9. Desperately apply to too many positions in one organization.

If you apply to more than two positions in an organization, it looks like a desperate move. They will assume you don't have any other options so you're applying everywhere. And nobody likes an obsessed stage five clinger. Don't be that person.

It also can look bad from the perspective that you

don't know what you want or you can't make a decision.

10. You only apply through an online job board.

After you upload your resume to an online job board, with the click of a button you can apply to as many companies as you desire. The only issue is, so can—and does—the rest of the world.

How many times have you won the mega-millions lottery? Your odds aren't much better on an online job board.

Don't be delusional like Lloyd Christmas, in Dumb and Dumber, when Mary Swanson tells him their chances of being together are one in a million. And he says, "So you're telling me there's a chance."

There are many other reasons resumes are ignored, but these ten are some of the most common mistakes.

The bottom line is finding an internship or job is hard. There are many moving pieces that are outside your control.

For example, even the mood of the resume reviewer at the time can effect if you get called for an interview.

However, you will make the job search easier by avoiding the mistakes above. Let other applicants, who don't read this book, make those errors while you increase your chances of getting hired.

> ☐ Quick tip: Before you finalize your resume, I recommend revisiting this list to use it as a checklist. This isn't a driver's test where if you fail, you can try again next week. You get one shot at applying to some organizations.

As you'll find out, one of my mottos is to capitalize on every possible advantage. Understanding why most resumes are ignored, and then following this information to improve your resume is another clear advantage.

We are only getting started on how you're going to stand out from the pack as a coveted applicant by multiple organizations.

Chapter 07

Your Extended Golden Resume

Some people believe that paper resumes will eventually be obsolete and replaced by digital resumes. I'm not a fortune teller, so I don't know if this is what the future holds or not.

But, I do know this: When you apply, you can safely bet each organization is searching your name on Google to see what they find.

This is why everything about you that people can find online is also your resume. Your Facebook profile is your resume. Your Twitter bio is your resume. Those photos of you at the bar are your resume. These online results are what I call your Extended

Golden Resume. And it's important to get it right.

All the information on the internet plays a role in the organization's opinion of you. Sometimes the information can be false or out of your control, but it's your loss since the company won't know the difference.

As I wrote in the previous chapter, a questionable internet presence is a top reason applicants are rejected. So, do not take your Extended Golden Resume lightly. It can build your reputation or ruin it.

Besides the party pictures and negative information, what's even more detrimental to you is if they search your name and find nothing. This raises questions about your trustworthiness, ambiguity, and lack of social network in a social network age. It's good to show a presence and familiarity with social media, but in a professional way.

So, will organizations find positive or negative results when they search your name? Will you get rejected because the search results turned up nothing?

Instead of risking a Google search branding you inaccurately, you can help yourself by taking control of your Extended Golden Resume. The best way to craft your own personal brand and digital resume is to create quality content where the recruiters can find it.

Here are four specific ways to do just that.

1. Engaged social media profiles.

Contributing thoughtful Twitter comments or Facebook posts to a discussion is one way to help your digital brand. These contributions will give the impression that you're connected in a network and can discuss topics in different areas.

Follow people who do work you want to do and people with the positions you want. And then, engage with them. Even if they don't respond, it will show you're in on the conversation.

But, I caution you to think long and hard before sending every tweet, comment, or post to the world. You don't want a heat of the moment feeling to permanently harm your reputation. Also, don't be one of those people that hasn't tweeted in two years or you can lose credibility and seem flakey.

If you think your social media profiles are minor in getting a job, you might want to consider these next findings.

Facebook is used by 66% of recruiters and Twitter is used by 54% of recruiters, according to theundercoverrecruiter.com. Odds are more likely than not that your recruiter is checking your Facebook and Twitter account.

2. Professional LinkedIn profile.

Also according to theundercoverrecruiter.com, 93% of companies use LinkedIn for recruiting. Yes, 93% and this number is most likely growing!

Because LinkedIn recruiting is so widespread, you first should make a LinkedIn profile, if you don't have one already. Then you need to put in effort so your profile showcases you in a positive light.

For starters, there are three main essentials to include. First, a professional looking photo of your face (in high resolution) is a must have since that will be your profile's first impression. A selfie, un-professional, or blurry photo is a terrible choice.

Second, write a concise and well-written summary describing what you're currently doing and what you're interested in working on in the future. The summary section is a great opportunity to share your passion and uniqueness with employers.

Third, provide an email address or phone number in the bottom of the summary section. After your dashing picture and well-written summary, they will want more information. So, give them a way to reach you at the end of your summary.

After finishing this book and updating your resume, simply copy and paste parts from your resume to LinkedIn for the experience, education, and projects—only link to these projects if they're truly quality work—sections of LinkedIn.

3. Write on Medium.com, or another platform.

A step up from maintaining positive, professional social media accounts is publishing your own content. If you don't want to deal with the hassle of setting up and running your own website, Medium.com is your solution.

Medium is a growing website with a clean design that makes every action super simple. Users can write content, upload pictures, and publish with ease in a matter of seconds.

Medium also gives writers easy opportunities to build a following by connecting with Facebook and Twitter accounts, and putting follow buttons on the stories you publish.

It also looks good to write stories for an online magazine, blog, or journal. Contributing content is an excellent move to gain more influence over the search results of your name.

Writing posts on someone else's website is effective, however it is not as effective as creating your own website.

4. Start your own blog or website.

Compared to the other options above, creating your own website takes more effort, but it certainly gives you the most value to your digital presence. With a blog, you now control the messages attached to your name.

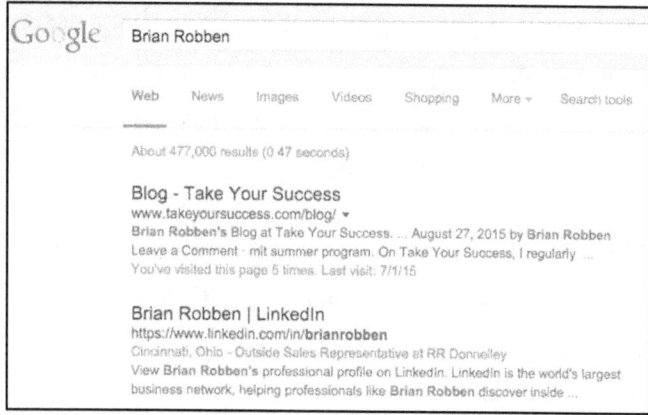

For example, if you type in 'Brian Robben' on Google, my website www.TakeYourSuccess.com shows up as the first result. (LinkedIn is second, followed by Twitter, Instagram, and Medium.com.) This means recruiters are going to see my website, and attach positive connotations.

Also, a blog is the perfect channel to position yourself as an authority in the industry by publishing quality content. You can write about trending topics in your market, your takeaways from new research, or make a thought-provoking argument to lead your online community's discussion.

These blog posts will also give you instant credibility, make you stand out from other applicants, and showcase your communication skills.

The recruiter's get the chance to feel like they know you better through your writing, and this creates the perception that you're less of a risk. We already discussed how much recruiters try to reduce risk in the hiring process.

I started Take Your Success after my job search, and missed all these benefits when I applied. I guarantee having a successful website on my resume would make my application cycle even better!

So a solid Extended Golden Resume is a necessity in this ultra-competitive digital age.

☐ Quick tip: If you put in this extra work, then your impressive digital resume will take pressure off of your normal resume. Plus, if the paper resume ever goes obsolete,

you'll have your own website to attach your resume.

Chalk this up as another advantage under your belt.
Of course, there are more advantages to come! But,
we need to ensure that no insecurities, doubts, and
fears get in your way.

Chapter 08

Your Mind Runs The Machine

You might think the job search is defined by what you write on your resume and what you say in your interviews. But you're missing the engine that drives the whole golden process.

Every success starts with what's at your core: your mind and your beliefs.

Applying to companies can be a vulnerable and intimidating process. You're explicitly being judged if you're good enough or not, and being judged is an uncomfortable feeling.

For example, it's similar to you being in a beauty

pageant. Except instead of you being exposed in a swimsuit competition where you're scrutinized in front of the judges, your exposed resume is scrutinized in front of the employer. Some might prefer the swimsuit in this case.

The doubts and fears of putting yourself out there to these organizations to only get rejected can sometimes cause you to not apply.

Or maybe you do apply, but you let the doubts and fears tell you you're out of your league and will never get the position. Then you interview poorly and it's a self-fulfilling prophecy.

But, have you considered another way of looking at this?

No one enjoys being judged and picked apart. I had insecurities in my job search. And Beyoncé had insecurities in her job search, says "her camp" Everyone has insecurities.

So, while they won't tell you, the job search is nerve-wracking for your competition, too.

Let's examine the most common limiting beliefs when writing your resume and interviewing.

1. I don't interview well.

Sure, you might have fumbled over your words before, said the wrong answer, or went speechless for ten seconds during an interview.

But, how can you say you don't interview well, when you haven't prepared effectively to interview well?

Interviewing is a craft that takes time and energy. It takes practice. No one is an instantly perfect interviewee!

After you finish this book, and follow the strategies, then come back and tell me you don't interview well.

2. I'm not interesting.

This is a tough one. What are you going to say when the interviewer says: "Tell me about yourself." If you go into this conversation thinking you have nothing to say, it won't be a good situation.

Believing your background isn't interesting will also cause you to write fluffy sentences on your resume that essentially mean nothing. But, the greater loss is these fluffy sentences will take up space you could use to write about your interesting story.

Trust me, your story is interesting. Do you know why? Because no one has experienced life in the same way you have. By default, you are the only one in the world with your personal story and so it will be brand new to the interviewer.

Believing you have something intriguing to say to recruiters will be essential in what's coming next in this book. And trust me, you do.

3. My GPA is too low.

Unless your GPA is below a minimum requirement for applicants, then don't let this thought minimize your job search. (If the requirement is a 3.5, and you're at 3.4 or even 3.3, I would still apply since it's close.)

In all the other situations, you can turn a low GPA into a positive by explaining that you didn't invest as much time studying because of other interests. You were busy finding what career you wanted to pursue, leading a student organization, building your professional network, or working to pay for your education.

4. I don't have the right major.

I read article after article about a liberal arts major excelling in a tech company, or vice versa. In this age, if you can show your ability to learn and produce value, the company will hire you.

For example, people told me an English major didn't belong in outside sales. But, I proved each one of them wrong using the strategies in the following chapters to get interviews and ultimately job offers.

Like the examples above, replace the limiting belief of not having the right major with a positive belief. Use the perspective that a different background helps you stand out.

Confidence Is Contagious

If you're at the interview stage, the interviewer will

immediately notice your confidence or lack of confidence.

If you're timid and think the job is too good for you, your facial expressions, the look in your eyes, and your body language will give your internal feelings away.

On the other hand, don't be cocky and think you're better than this person or that will be clear, too.

> ☐ Quick tip: Look at the interview as a meeting of equals, where you offer your working ability and they offer you the position and salary. Let your confidence be contagious.

Once you overcome your limiting beliefs and grow your confidence, you'll be unstoppable in what I tell you next.

Chapter 09

Your Own Personal Marketing Strategy

Well, you made it! You've made it through the necessary background information, and now we will turn toward resume and interview greatness.

Before we talk about the golden resume, we have to talk about marketing. I know, you thought you were done with background information. Well, this isn't background information. This is information that goes on your resume and in your every job-seeking movement.

Do you know that major companies, like Apple and

Disney, spend billions of dollars a year on advertisements for their marketing? These expenses alone are a testament to the importance of marketing.

As these companies realize marketing is key to their success, you should also recognize that the way you market yourself will be the difference between failure and success.

If you see resume building as a marketing strategy, you'll already be ahead of your competition.

The good news is that I found that almost no one puts their resume in the mental frame of a personal marketing strategy. So when you do think that way, you'll be the one who gets extraordinary results.

There are four marketing strategies to separate yourself from the competition: 1) play against type, 2) don't undersell yourself, 3) make every word count, and 4) tell powerful stories. Let's get started.

1. Play Against Type

Playing against type is simply the process of figuring out what stereotypes a hiring manager likely has about you, and then going against those assumptions in your resume.

Going against the common assumption will make you standout as a refreshing option compared to all the applicants who appear the same. But first, you need to determine what the assumptions are about your background, based on the position.

Here's an example from my own life. I applied to outside sales positions as an English major. As you probably know, English majors get the perception of being introverted romantic thinkers, who only read and write but don't get things done.

After identifying the assumptions the recruiter or manager has about English majors, I turned what some would see as a disadvantage into my ultimate advantage.

I focused my efforts on communicating the opposite of what they believed about English majors—as you'll see in the chapter where I show you my resume. (And these character traits are true about me, so it wasn't difficult. Don't lie or this tactic won't work.) In playing against type, I persuaded them that my studies in English align perfectly with sales.

To tackle the introvert stereotype (which doesn't go well with sales), I showed my outgoing personality in my resume and interviews. They also likely assumed I had my head in the clouds, so I communicated my fierce competitiveness. When they questioned if I could only read and write, I provided evidence of my excellent salesmanship and success in other positions.

With this being said, I don't want you to get confused and think I played down my English major. My ability to communicate, critically read and write well are some of my main skills, so I didn't avoid talking about those. And in the same light, you shouldn't play down a part of you so you can play against type. Playing against type doesn't involve self-deprecation, but showing yourself in a different light than other applicants. Tell them what they don't assume about you and play up what they might already expect.

I relayed how my studies in English applied almost identically to sales. I shared how both roles require targeting a primary audience, communicating a message to them, and persuading them to find your point agreeable based on evidence.

I challenged their previous assumption of English majors. And then, I more importantly differentiated from business majors by detailing how my degree actually prepared me to succeed in a sales role more than other majors.

The recruiters and hiring managers ate it up!

If you can effectively play against the common assumptions made of people in your major or school, you will appear versatile and intriguing. Organizations absolutely love versatile candidates because almost no job is singular in its responsibility.

Plus, companies hold versatile applicants in high regard as they forecast these candidates transitioning smoothly in promotions and leadership roles.

2. Don't Underrate Yourself

Being modest and humble has no place when it comes to your resume and interview strategy. When you're meeting your significant other's parents, then you can use this modest card, but not with a dream job on the line.

With intense competition and limited job opportunities, you only get in your own way if your resume undersells yourself.

I say this because too many times people leave out incredible experiences or achievements that they believe isn't relevant to the position. But, in reality, the interviewer would die to know this fact and it could completely change their perspective of you.

For one, interesting facts like getting 250,000 YouTube hits, writing a book, or interviewing someone famous, will all help the interviewer see you as more of an interesting person.

This will open the door for them to ask follow up questions and begin an engaging conversation. Now you're connecting with the interviewer so they get to know you and can see you fit in well with their organization. Also, these details help you stay longer in their memory due to their uniqueness.

So, don't leave interesting details off of your resume, and certainly don't omit these details and then bring them up in an interview. The recruiter will think you weren't smart enough to include it on your resume.

If you're asking where do these details fit, a good location is at the bottom of your resume in a new section titled Additional Information. More on that later.

3. Make Every Word Count

You want to think of your resume as one notecard that your teacher allows you to write anything you want on it to use for the exam. Are you going to waste space by using unhelpful words? No, you're not.

For a better resume, and since we are going to commit to one-page, it's in your best interest to make every word contribute value. Concise, clear resume writing will give you more space to play against type and properly market yourself.

Too many times resume writers use fluffy words

and phrases that they think sound impressive or sophisticated, but really these lines have no true meaning to the narrative. The recruiter immediately thinks you don't know how to communicate well, or your past experiences are so weak that you had nothing better to include.

And when these words contribute no meaning, space is wasted where interesting details and experiences could have revealed something golden. Don't waste precious space with duds of words. Think of every word as a precious, golden element. When you write nonsense, you ultimately trade impressing the resume reviewer for wasting their time and your chance at the job.

☐ Quick tip: Passive voice often requires more words. So, use active voice to make every word count and keep the reader interested.

Basically, be interesting, be brilliant, and be concise.

The fourth marketing strategy, storytelling, is so important it needed its own chapter. Let's keep the momentum going!

Chapter 10

Stories Win Interviews
And Job Offers

Before we get into this interview strategy, I want to first ask you a few questions.

What's your favorite book? What's your favorite movie? What makes you laugh the most?

I don't know your favorite book, your favorite movie, or the specific thing that makes you laugh the most. But, I can answer those three questions with 100% accuracy.

The answer is... the best STORY!

The reason a book is your favorite is because you love the book's narrative, which attaches you to the well-being of the characters. Your favorite movie has the best plot line and brings out all your emotions. And when you hear a really funny story, you erupt in uncontrollable laughter.

We keep reading, watching, and listening because we want to know what happens next.

You might ask: what's the relevance to your resume? The point is this: You want to create a story that keeps your interview interesting and that has your interviewers asking: what happens next? Spoiler alert: you get hired!

Let me explain this in the context of the interviewer's mindset. This person wants to find an employee that will contribute value, but they also are looking for a good personality fit.

After interviewing 12 different candidates with similar resumes and backgrounds, who say similar buzzwords about being hard working, motivated, and organized, this interviewer is bored out of their mind.

If you walk in and give the same talk about why you're hard working, motivated, and organized, the interviewer is going to politely nod their head. But, their internal voice will say, "Not again. Is this over yet?" They aren't thinking: "What happens next in the story?"

In other words, you most likely won't be successful because you failed to connect with the interviewer.

But, say you walk in to the interview with a powerful personal narrative that is clear from your resume.

Then, in your interview, what you say and the examples you tell also relate directly to your narrative.

Now you will gain the interviewer's attention and more questions will be thrown your way. Your collection of other stories bring your resume to life!

The interviewer is enjoying the conversation to a high degree and so the interview moves from an interrogation to a casual conversation.

Because of your amazing stories that showcase your ability to produce and likeable personality, your name is placed at the top of the hiring list.

The lesson here is if you can tell a good story, you have a huge upper hand over the other applicants who choose not to tell narratives, or cannot communicate them well.

Why are stories so influential? Because stories have the power to change our mood, what we believe, and what we do.

Stories stick with people because the listener attaches emotions as the plot advances, and can actually experience the story like it happened to them. It's the same reason your favorite movie or book has stuck in your memory. The interviewer will easily remember your name and face if your stories are effective.

Storytelling has influential power over the interviewer's mood, beliefs about you as an applicant, and his or her actions moving forward.

Let Your Resume Guide Your Interview

We drilled the concept of having a clear personal narrative as a candidate. However, an advanced candidate will also take the power of storytelling to another level by including storytelling elements for each resume line.

Come up with quick, specific stories for each part of your resume. Make sure you have an arsenal of around 15 personal stories that provide convincing examples of your successes and resume experiences.

And since no interview is a pop quiz, you can prepare as much as you need to naturally tell these stories.

Practice telling these narratives to yourself in the mirror. Or record your stories on your phone or computer, and then play them back to make improvements. But, don't memorize them word for word, or it'll come out fake when you interview. Tell the story like you'd tell your mom.

Getting your compelling stories down is a huge xfactor since most interviews go down two paths.

In the first scenario, the person interviewing you will go down your resume from top to bottom and ask questions as he or she goes along. Since you have multiple stories for each position, your game plan of creating a narrative will allow you to crush this interview.

In the second common scenario, the interviewer will ask you behavioral based questions that could be all over the place. Questions like:

- What is your proudest moment in college, and why?
- Why are you interested in a sales position?
- When's a time you went above and beyond expectations?

But, you attack these questions the same way as the first scenario. With your arsenal of prepared stories and resume in front of you, you will ace these questions. Don't think of these questions as a way to trip you up. Think of them as a way to tell your story. No matter how the interviewer asks, you want to get the same points across.

Example Questions And Answers

Great stories start with context, move to action, and finish with the result. If it helps you, think of the acronym CAR (C for context, A for action, and R for result). These answers should be around 30 seconds to a minute each.

What follows are example questions and answers you can use as a model for your stories. Some of these answers are average and not that memorable. Pay attention to the golden answers—they will make an impression.

Example question: What is your proudest moment in college, and why?

Average answer: "I would say my position as president of my fraternity. That was a really great experience. I love all the people I've met and what I've learned. Those memories will stay with me forever."

Golden answer: "Oh, that's an easy answer! Being president of my fraternity is without a doubt my proudest achievement. And it's not because of the title, but how I got there.

So, I actually ran for president as a sophomore. I knew I wanted to be a leader and give back to this fraternity that gave me so much confidence, so much community, and so many good times. But, I lost the election for president. Part of me was upset and angry that I didn't get the position.

But, then I decided that being upset wasn't going to make me any happier or serve any positive purpose. So, I asked my fraternity brothers for honest feedback about why they voted for the other person, and they basically said he seemed more involved in fraternity events.

I decided to take their feedback to heart and step up that year, so I became super involved in my fraternity's philanthropy and organized my frat's alumni weekend. I actually increased the number of alumni coming back by 23 people based on my email campaign. Then, I ran for president my junior year and got elected president. The journey to getting elected president is what makes it my greatest achievement."

Example question: Why are you interested in a sales

position?

Average answer: "I love sales. My dad is in sales and I decided that I wanted to follow his footsteps because I've seen how successful he's been and want to achieve similar results. Also, I'm very competitive and realize sales requires a competitive drive."

Golden answer: "I believe I'm a great fit for sales because I'm both an extremely competitive person and I'm an extremely outgoing person. For example, I'm so competitive that I didn't let two of my really good friends join my intramural basketball team because I wanted to win so badly.

I said something like sorry guys, it's nothing personal but we want to win the championship this year and I don't know if we could play as well with such a big roster. I later massaged these relationships, and we won the intramural basketball championship.

And the second example is that I love talking to people and building relationships. Many times when I go to my friends' house I'll talk to their parents and just learn about what they do. My friends think it's weird when I do this, but I just naturally enjoy hearing people's stories. My interest in people helps me develop relationships, which is crucial in sales because people do business with people they like.

So I feel that my personality is best aligned with sales. That's why I'm only applying to sales positions, and nothing else."

Example question: When's a time you went above and beyond expectations?

Average answer: "In my journalism class, the teacher asked for a PowerPoint presentation on the Korean War. I went above and beyond by not doing a PowerPoint, but interviewing someone from the Korean War and made it into a video. I received an A+. It was awesome."

Golden answer: "In my journalism class last semester, the final project required a PowerPoint presentation on the Korean War. I wanted to do something different and excellent based on my appreciation for this amazing journalism teacher.

So, I did some research and made some phone calls

until I found a 1st Marine who served in Korea. Then I called this Marine and explained my idea to interview him for my project. I found out he was in Kentucky, only a couple hours away from me in Oxford, Ohio. So I went down there and interviewed this man who won a Purple Heart as a machine gunner. He shared heart-wrenching stories like how his two best friends died and his personal thoughts about the war.

Then I edited the video and showed it in class. My project went so well that the teacher pulled her chair next to the screen as she watched. She had a big smile on her face at the end for how we honored this man. I received an A+, but when I look back on this experience my grade is the last thing that comes to mind."

Many people don't tell stories when they answer questions. However, when you tell stories you show your personality—in a positive light—which can matter more than your technical skills!

☐ Quick tip: People do business with people they like. They certainly hire those they like. And everyone loves good stories, because they are a connecting force.

By connecting with the interviewer in your story-telling, the recruiter will have a clear narrative of you as a candidate and their memory of you will be strong, instead of forgotten the next day.

Through capturing their mind, you will beat out other candidates and win the job offer!

Chapter 11

The Resume Rules

You now have the firepower in your marketing strategy to write a powerful resume and dominate interviews.

However, you will also need to craft what you learned into an organized and functional resume. The following Resume Rules will help you actually write your resume. I know what you're thinking: finally!

Since there are many competing opinions out there when it comes to writing a resume, I'm going to include the obvious and less-obvious rules that work. Simply having a professional resume that follows these rules will set you apart from other applicants, and every advantage counts.

1. Modify each resume for jobs in different fields.

You will not stand out by using a general resume to apply to different jobs in different fields, which shows a lack of personal positioning. Instead, write specific evidence based on your experience that explains how you can contribute value to this specific organization. (Also, a specialized resume will serve you well in the interview process.)

In other words, if you're only applying to accounting jobs, then you can keep the same resume. But, if you're applying to accounting and marketing positions, you'll want two different resumes: one version customized to your accounting ability and experience, and the second version customized to your marketing ability and experience.

Next, look at the organization's website to cater your resume. Soak in their mission statement, purpose, core strengths, and other pages. This will give you a better understanding of what they value, and assist you in writing similar keywords to get the recruiter's attention. Also, write common keywords you see in the job description.

2. Use a simple Word document.

A resume template or table format is designed to save you time. But, when I experimented with these shortcuts (for this book), I found more problems than help.

Spacing and organization can actually be incredibly frustrating and inefficient as you wrestle with the program to do what you want.

Also, if an employer views your resume on a different device (their phone, tablet, or computer), they could see funky spacing, paragraphs cut off, and messy organization. A nightmare you don't have time for!

Instead, prepare your resume on a standard Word document. (I say Word over Google because of its superior formatting options, at this point.) Then, to avoid any formatting issues, save the Word document as a PDF. So you can submit or email your resume with confidence that the formatting won't change.

3. Don't include an objective.

Employers are much more concerned with their objective—finding an employee with a good personality fit and who can contribute value—than your objective. If you apply for the position, then your objective is clearly to get the job.

Another point is if you right a solid objective that fits the company, then you only did what you're supposed to. But, many times people write an objective that isn't exactly what the company is looking for, and the recruiter will use this to weed out applicants.

Don't forget these reviewers get flooded with resumes, so you won't want to give them any ammunition to reject you.

4. Organization expresses importance.

Since people read top to bottom, place the section first where you have the most relevant experiences and impressive results to hook the interviewer on your narrative. Spend significant time driving in these details and the applicable skills you learned. Then put the next most relevant section second, and so on.

It's a risk to put key points near the bottom of the resume because they may never be brought up or you may run out of time.

5. Spacing to win.

For your work experience section, the conventional way of thinking is to use reverse chronological order to list your most recent job first, and then go backwards from there. However, I found the better strategy is to list the most relevant job—to the position you're applying to—first in your work experience section.

Because the first position in your work experience usually receives the most attention, the recruiter will see this job and be more likely to grant you an interview.

Then, you can drive the discussion in the interview

as you communicate the skills, results, and experience you gained, and how it translates well to the job you're interviewing for.

If you list your work experiences in chronological order, you might miss the opportunity to "play your best card" if it's in the second or third position.

To qualify the statement above, if you're putting a less recent position above a more recent one, make sure it is in a reasonable timeframe. Don't place a job you did three years ago, because it's slightly more relevant, ahead of a position you had a year ago.

6. Stick to a one-page resume.

The people who read your resume are extremely busy zipping through hundreds or thousands of documents, and you want to dump a second page on to them?

If you follow the story-telling strategy, you will remember that you need to address and back up every experience on your resume with supporting stories. In other words, adding a second page opens the door for many additional questions that you'll need to prepare for—not a strategic and not a fun move.

Plus, anything longer than one page can give the impression you can't be concise and make decisions, so you quickly threw everything on two pages. Only later in your career will you potentially need to expand to two pages.

7. Stats are sexy.

What looks more appealing to you in these two examples: "Increased revenue compared to the previous summer," or "Drove revenue by 173% and personally acquired 13 new customer accounts"? Of course, the second example looks better.

When you have the chance to, always quantify. If your numbers are extremely impressive, bold the font to get the reviewer's attention. People are drawn to things they can measure.

Positive stats ease two concerns of recruiters, because they signal you will succeed in their company and you're less of a risk. If you don't have the specific numbers, explain their importance to your previous boss to get these figures.

8. Utilize simple fonts and designs.

Be unique in the content of your resume and how you interview, not the font or design of your resume. There's little value added with complex fonts and designs if they go right, and significant value lost if they go wrong.

☐ Quick tip: Simple fonts and designs protect you from uploading to the applicant system and ending up with an unreadable resume. Cambria, Georgia, Trebuchet MS, and Verdana are easy-to-read fonts for resume reviewers on both print and a digital screen. (Get away from the boring Arial and Times New Roman fonts.)

In addition, too many lines on a page going vertical and horizontal can be a distraction. If you're applying for a graphic design or art-related position, then this rule is a different story for you and you'll want to show some of your skills.

9. Eliminate fluffy words with zero meaning.

Fluffy words and phrases that express no meaning only take up space and cause you to leave behind interesting details that can impress the reviewer.

For example, consider this resume line under a work experience position, "Worked to increase and develop excellent customer service for great results."

What are you talking about dude? Do you know how to write a resume? Clearly not. Keep reading.

There's wasted words (get rid of "Worked to increase and," by writing "Developed"). You wasted space since excellent and great results mean the same thing. And the results aren't qualified at all. What does great results mean?

This point relates directly back to the marketing strategy of making every word count.

10. Be careful with personal information and no photos.

The employer wants to know if you're a strong candidate. It's completely unnecessary to include your religious affiliation, sexual orientation, and political preference.

Even including smaller personal details could dismiss you from an interview. For example, say you write you love country towns in your personal details and the job you're applying for is in New York City, it could be seen as the wrong fit. Or you say your favorite thing to do is travel, but the job you applied for is strictly a desk job involving zero travel. They will question your interest in the position. You meant no harm, but both of these examples are red flags.

Every detail communicates something to the recruiter or hiring manager, so make these words relevant and positive. If you do add personal information, make sure it's directly tied to your resume's narrative.

For the super majority of jobs, don't include a personal picture on your resume. Photos are neither relevant nor professional in the job search. Save it for those Instagram likes.

11. Review spelling, grammar, formatting, and omissions with hawk-like precision.

Passing a program's spell check and grammar check tool isn't enough. Those tools are traps that create false confidence of your resume being accurate, when many times it contains errors.

☐ Quick tip: Spell check tools recognize if words are spelled correctly, but often can't determine if they are used properly (for example, *there* and *their*). The English language is so complex that grammar tools sometimes mark perfect usage as incorrect, and mark correct usage with errors.

If you would feel better doing it, start with using these tools. But, realize computers can only go so far, and the final accuracy test is on your shoulders.

So, review your resume and be razor sharp.

Pro-tips for editing include printing a physical copy, running line by line with a pen, looking up the spelling of bigger or unfamiliar words, and reading out loud.

Also, review the spacing, formatting, accuracy of dates, and don't leave off anything important. Then give it to a professor or friend and say: point out any errors you see.

The extra time spent reviewing your resume can save you from blowing your chances at a next round interview.

12. Special paper isn't special.

If you're bringing a physical copy to a career fair, information night, or interview, just use standard white computer paper. For one, the person who receives your resume could start focusing on the special paper's texture, rather than the text on the document.

Two, I've seen people waste thirty minutes to one hour going from grocery store to print shop to find special paper the night before an interview. Avoid confusing fake productivity (spending time getting special resume paper) with real productivity (spending time preparing for the interview).

We are making good progress so far. Next, we are going to view and analyze my resume.

Chapter 12

Analyzing My Resume

Now I'm going to walk you through the resume I used to apply for full-time sales jobs almost a year ago. Since I've researched and learned more about resumes, I would make changes to my resume if I could go back.

But, at that time I still executed many strategies and gained huge advantages over my peers. My resume performed excellent to the tune of many job offers, plus a high salary that I'm still getting rewarded for to this day.

BRIAN J. ROBBEN

robbenbj@miamioh.edu

329 West Church St., Oxford, OH 45056

EDUCATION

MIAMI UNIVERSITY, Oxford, OH   2011-2015
- B.A. in English Professional Writing and a minor in community-based leadership.
- Coursework includes public writing, rhetoric, leadership, communication, and analytical research.
- Overall GPA: **3.96/4.0** Major GPA: **4.0/4.0**
- Completing honors senior thesis about the evolution of Major League Baseball reporting in different mediums.

WORK EXPERIENCE

Student Fundraiser Representative, **RUFFALOCODY**, Oxford, OH   2013
- Personally acquired 333 pledges and a total of $33,690.50 for the Miami University Annual Fund, which supports endowment and student scholarships.
- Finished in fifth place out of 94 employees in total revenue.
- Achieved a 32.3% credit card gift rate when the premier office goal was 30%.

Summer Law Intern, **HAMILTON COUNTY PROSECUTOR'S OFFICE**, Cincinnati, OH   2012-14
- State of Ohio v. Donald Harvey Project- Personally responsible for orally and visually briefing administrators on the 1987 28-count-indictment case of serial killer Donald Harvey. Direct report to the prosecutor.
- Wrote discovery files for criminal cases to aid the prosecution process.

Writer, Researcher, **MOVE GUIDES**, London, United Kingdom   2013
- Curated three 45-page city guides for expatriates in international relocation to Orlando, FL; Minneapolis, MN; and Columbus, OH. Detailed local real estate markets, neighborhoods, culture, services, and attractions.

Baseball Umpire, **KINGS SPORTS, LLC.**, Cincinnati, OH   2007-2014
- Umpired 5-7 year olds (2007), promoted to umpire Division 1 (2009), second promotion to umpire the selective American Amateur Baseball Congress (AABC) of 13-16 year olds (2011).

CAMPUS ACTIVITY

President, **AMICUS CURIAE PRE-LAW SOCIETY**   2014-present
- On pace to increase the total number of members, speakers for our general body meetings, and networking events by 200% compared to the previous year.
- Lead executive board meetings and general body meetings to target members' benefit.

President, **SCOTT HALL COMMUNITY COUNCIL**   2012-2013
- Managed a $1,600 budget to provide programs that cater to the interests and needs of Scott Hall residents.
- Proposed and executed a weekend trip to build community rapport with 21 Scott Hall residents by attending the 2013 Miami vs. Notre Dame Hockey City Classic game at Soldier Field in Chicago, IL.

ADDITIONAL INFORMATION

- Biweekly opinion staff writer for *The Miami Student*, the oldest university newspaper in the United States.
- Staff writer for *Miami Quarterly*, a magazine published four times a year with hard deadlines.
- Captained an undefeated championship in the most competitive division of intramural basketball (2013).
- Merit honors recipient: Department of Geology and Environmental Earth Science Award - one of only two people awarded out of the 185 students in the course section, Clark Family Scholarship, Alumni Association Merit Scholarship, Leroy S. Galvin Memorial Scholarship and RedHawk Excellence Scholarship.

Why Did My Resume Work So Well?

I created my narrative around being a:

- "Expert communicator and persuader," based on my studies in rhetoric and communication. This tells the hiring manager that I know how to identify a specific audience, construct an argument with support based on their assumptions, and persuade this audience to take a favorable action. These are the fundamentals of sales and I wanted to show them I knew that.

- "Brilliant learner and achiever," based on my near-perfect GPA. I wrote that in bold type. This communicates that I can quickly learn the job and produce fast results for the organization.

- "Intensely competitive, go-getter salesman," based on my success finishing in 5th place out of 94 employees at RuffaloCODY, my writing position for MOVE Guides where I sold the expatriates on each city, and captaining the undefeated basketball championship (this is a nutty detail but it worked

for me and started great interview conversations).

Using the experiences in my resume, I designed these narratives for what I wanted the recruiters and hiring managers to think about me. Then in the interview, in case it wasn't clear, I drove home each point through stories for outstanding results.

Also, do you see how I "played against type"? Most candidates applying for sales have a business background, and sales recruiters see little to no English majors each year. So although my resume is littered with writing positions, I used my writing experiences as an advantage in my resume and interviews.

Ok, now it's time for the specific breakdown of my resume.

EDUCATION

My education section looks standard from the start, where I detail the usual suspects like everyone else: school, school's location, dates attending, and my major plus minor.

Then, we get to the part where I start to break away

from the pack to say, "Hey, look at me hiring manager. I'm different, and I'm interesting."

In the second bullet, I write, "Coursework includes public writing, rhetoric, leadership, communication, and analytical research." Absolutely no resume I saw did this!

I added this line to proactively attack the stereotype of an English major. I knew I needed to get these recruiters away from the thoughts of me sitting on a cloud like a loner, as I wrote romantic poems for four years with no real-world skills. So, I took my opportunity to prove them wrong right from the get-go.

They would expect public writing and communication, but not the other three words from an English major.

I wrote "rhetoric" to show my studies in persuasion and Aristotle's three methods of persuasion (logic, emotions, and credibility), which again goes back to my narrative and a message that translates well to the sales industry.

I used "leadership" because of my minor in community-based leadership. Almost every company values effective leadership, and it's also not a common field for English majors.

I included "analytical research" to show my experience using critical thinking, making detailed inferences, and analyzing comparisons. This again is not stereotyped with English majors, so I played against type here, too.

When you write your resume, choose these coursework words carefully so they align with what you studied and the responsibilities of the job you want. I couldn't add sales, because I didn't explicitly study sales, but ideally that word would have been in my coursework section.

Then, I bolded the font of my GPA, which separates me from the competition since it's a top 1% grade point average. I did this to make sure that a recruiter would never fail to see it.

The last bullet in this section is my senior thesis, which was in progress at this time. I thought about expanding to a second line, but I gave the recruiters enough information to spark their interest. Then I explained more in my interview, if they asked about it.

☐ Quick tip: That brings up another point. If you're in the middle of a project, don't feel like you can't add it to your resume until it's finished. Once you start, throw it on your resume because it will likely be an easy interview talking point since you're presently in the thick of it.

WORK EXPERIENCE

If you looked at my resume closely, you may have noticed that my first work experience role occurred in 2013 and my second ended in 2014. Isn't that backwards? Yes, it is. But, I designed it this way.

To stay proactive in my personal marketing pitch, and convince the hiring managers that I had what it takes in sales, I put my best sales experience first. I disregarded the standard reverse chronological order (and I'm sure some resume experts disagree agree with it), but it worked beautifully.

To capitalize on their fleeting attention, I hit them with hard figures of acquiring 333 pledges and $33,690.50 in around 12 months. This showed that I'm not only an achiever in the classroom, but I can achieve in a working environment, too.

Although it wasn't technically a sales position, since we were asking for pledges and not selling a product or service, I told these people a story of my experience.

I told hiring managers, "We started with calling scripts when speaking to alumni and parents. But, they sounded robotic and made it difficult to emotionally connect to the other person.

So, I decided to ditch the script and do a more natural call asking deeper questions about their times in college. I ended up learning about wild parties and stories of how people awkwardly met their spouse. After gaining the alumni's trust, the money I brought in soared.

Then I told recruiters that my competitive determination to get better caused me to ask the number one caller what he did to be so successful. I took notes from him and used these in my calls.

These details showed the employer that I could adjust to get better, use my skills in English to communicate with people, and compete to get results.

Then, I pushed further. I told recruiters I wasn't satisfied with finishing fifth out of 94, and if I had more time I believe I would've been first. Again, this was to show my strong competitive trait.

I also would add to the competitive narrative by relaying what my housemate Jeff once told me, "Brian, you're the most competitive person I've ever met." Sure, this is a short comment, but it soaks in the interviewer's memory more than me simply telling them that I'm competitive.

Here's another thing to pay attention to. For the student fundraiser position on my resume, I offered three bullet points, and no other position got that much text with it. I did this because this experience aligned best with sales and I needed to play it up as much as possible.

Alright, let's move on to my second work experience position as a summer law intern.

In describing this position, I use two words: personally responsible. Why? I want to communicate that I executed my individual responsibilities of researching, reporting, and presenting to the head prosecutor on my findings.

I'm also adding to my narrative of "expert communicator and persuader" by detailing how I "orally and visually" presented the material for the prosecutor's review. Do you notice how I also made the subject of what I worked on interesting?

These recruiters didn't meet any other candidates that worked on a serial killer case, and this started another excellent story if the conversation happened to go down that path.

I finished the first bullet point with "direct report to the prosecutor" to communicate my clear role and successful outcome. "Direct report" also sounds more impressive than if I had said, "reported to the prosecutor."

The second bullet point under summer law intern describes more of my general responsibilities, and adds to the fact that I didn't simply get my manager coffee and I didn't do paperwork. Instead, I explained how my job was vital to the prosecution process. That idea adds to my overall impression.

The next position, titled writer and researcher for MOVE Guides, helped me stand out. I worked for a startup company in London and this fact is very uncommon among other applicants.

It also adds to my desired narrative as a "go-getter salesman." I achieved this by sharing with the recruiter how I actively sought after this position and had to convince a woman through Skype that although I wasn't from Orlando, FL, I could research and do such an excellent job that everyone would assume I was a local.

I finally convinced her to give me the opportunity and received rave reviews for my first city guide. I also received $400, which I told recruiters to show the worth of the project.

A few months later, I wanted two more freelance

jobs. The manager was hesitant again since I had never lived in Minneapolis, MN or Columbus, OH. I told her the first city guide went so well that she could trust me, and then I delivered two more 45-page documents.

This story is really impressive to recruiters.

One thing to note: I chose the word curated, because it's more attractive and holds more weight than the saying "wrote" or "compiled." I told you I'm a resume nerd!

Last in this work experience section is my umpire position. Some of you might question the relevance, but it served two very important roles on my resume.

First, the umpire position supports the story of me being an "achiever," as I detail two quick promotions. Some people see umpiring as a difficult, unenviable position because of having to make close calls and having to handle the unruly emotions of crazy fans and coaches. I hoped these reviewers would see that I succeed under pressure.

Second, if I can umpire on the weekends for seven straight summers, it shows I have loyalty and that I'm likely to stay with their organization for an extended time if they hire me.

This message is important because a key pain point of recruiters is hiring someone, only to see them shortly take off for another company. So, I lessened this risk in their eyes with my long tenure as an umpire.

Plus, and more of a side note, I included this activity because it shows I'm down to earth in working with people and enjoying baseball. I didn't want to come off as an unrelatable super freak and library worm based off of my GPA and senior thesis.

CAMPUS ACTIVITY

I exemplify my leadership experience in the next two roles under campus activity. If you have leadership experience, it's highly valuable for recruiters and hiring managers.

Anyway, with my position as president of Pre-Law

Society, I detailed how I was on pace to double previous effort in members, speakers, and networking events. This goes to the "achiever" narrative in that I'm doing more with my resources. I also communicate my responsibility to run a meeting every week, with either my exec team, or the general body members.

Second in this section is my position as president of Scott Hall Community Council, which also showcases my leadership experience.

Numbers are always good qualifiers, so I detail the $1,600 budget where I allocated funds strategically to put on programs for the residents. This fact helps me play against type, because most recruiters and hiring managers would assume an English major doesn't do well with math and numbers.

My second point ties into the first bullet point as I give an example of a program I put on for the residents. With this, I often tell the story of a trip I organized to Chicago. I navigated multiple moving parts, and I succeeded by organizing people, our van transportation, and our Chicago hotel so we could explore the city and enjoy a hockey game together.

Do you see the word choice again? I used "proposed and executed" instead of "took a trip" or some other lame words that won't have the same impressive effect.

(Honestly, this position isn't that fancy, as I basically signed up for it and no one opposed me in an election format. But, recruiters and hiring managers don't know that. Wink.)

ADDITIONAL INFORMATION

The first two lines in this section detail my out of the classroom writing experience, more for reinforcement of my communication prowess than anything else.

In the first position, I only added "the oldest university newspaper in the United States" because I had extra space to fill out that line, plus it adds credibility. If adding this information had carried over to two lines, then I wouldn't have added it.

For the second bullet, I made sure the recruiter recognized that I had to properly prepare and organize for hard deadlines that couldn't be missed. Organization is crucial in the working world.

Moving to the third line, I made another calculated risk by including intramural basketball. I did this because it sparked good conversation, as did baseball, since sports are usually an easy talking point for many people.

And, again, this undefeated season and championship supports the "achiever" and "competitive" narrative of my marketing strategy.

The final bullet point in this section is the academic scholarships. In interviews, I would point out that the geology scholarship, where I beat out geology majors, is an example of me being a fast learner.

Every organization prefers fast learners over slow learners.

This award also communicates that I don't only perform well in English classes, so I'm versatile.

Overview

Like I said, if I could go back, I would change some things from my resume. And I definitely could have used more sales experience (which I would have done if I didn't plan on going to law school my freshmen year up to the start of my senior year).

The key takeaway here is crafting your resume to tell your story and communicate your personal marketing strategy.

To take you from the top of the mountain to the highest tip of the mountain, you need one last crucial insight. Keep reading!

Chapter 13

One Final Job Search Essential

If you follow all the previous strategies, and skip this chapter, you will be ahead of the majority of your peers.

But, by doing the following actions, you'll be in the top 1% of candidates and relatively ensure that you will have a successful job search cycle.

We are almost done. Listen up and finish strong, so no obstacle gets in your way.

Sometimes no matter how amazing your resume is the recruiter or hiring manager ultimately won't see it and you won't get an interview.

To counter this, how can you ensure they will see your resume and give you an interview? What else do you need?

Networking!

Network like a crazy person in your job search. Call everyone in your family and extended family. Talk to your parents, siblings, and relatives. Ask them if they have any connections in the industry you're applying to or general job search advice.

Chat with your friends, their parents, and neighbors to explain what you're looking for and how grateful you would be if they could introduce you to someone in the industry.

Call your previous classmates, colleagues, and alumni. Mention your mission to everyone near and far. At some point, that will lead to another conversation or meeting people in unusual ways.

Don't stop there! Find the hiring manager's information on LinkedIn and contact them directly. Call the specific companies where you've applied and talk about your interest. Or, ask to set up a meeting and this will clearly communicate your commitment to get an interview.

Ask a current employee out to coffee, and find out what they did to get the position. See if these employees have suggestions. Ask people for advice, not jobs. Plenty of people want to give advice, but have reservations about promising a job to so-and-so.

When searching every possible avenue, odds are someone knows someone who can help you out in a big way! For example, your mom's friend might not be able to help you out, but your mom's friend knows someone who works where you want a job, and has agreed to speak with you on the phone.

What's even better in many circumstances? Your newfound connection will have more power in the organization than a recruiter. So, when this superior asks a recruiter to give you a shot, you will sometimes jump all the applicants and to get an interview.

And the advantage doesn't stop there. You will also improve your chances of getting the job because this respected superior is vouching that you're a good fit for the company and will succeed. This puts the thought in the recruiter's mind that you're a low risk and if you fail, it's not the recruiter's fault.

As you will find out, the power of networking is fair to those who use it, and unfair to those who don't. Put in the effort, and you will get opportunities far beyond uploading your resume to an online form.

Send Off

Entering a job search can be taxing and difficult as you manage the other responsibilities in your life with this time-consuming process.

After spending hours on your resume and finding powerful stories, you might be tempted to stop there and feel like you've done enough.

However, if you can't get interviews, then all your resume and interview work may go to waste.

This picture will help you understand the point above: Imagine yourself stuck in a dark cave without direction (the job search process). In this cave, you have a powerful flashlight (your resume) and a strategic map (your marketing interview strategy), but if you can't find the tunnel to get started (receive the interview), then your flashlight and map are useless.

So we need to get interviews to reach the stage where we can show off our golden resume and powerful interview strategy.

How do you do this? Don't just passively send resumes online.

First, push through to network like crazy so you can relax at the end of this process. The key ingredients for powering through to success are unapologetic networking mixed with determination, persistence, and preparation.

Second, mentally prepare for rejection because it's part of the process! Once you get past the fear of rejection, you will free yourself to go at this job search with unmatched energy and then unmatched results.

Once you do get the interview, blow them away with

your resume and the strategies we have discussed.

By using networking and these strategies, your worst problem may be deciding between too many good job offers!

Chapter 14

Take Your Success

Congratulations, you finished reading this book! You're now set to take these strategies and your major competitive advantage to write your golden resume.

If you follow this book to a tee, I guarantee you'll succeed in your job search.

These strategies have helped countless top performers and myself get amazing results, which we continue to capitalize on today.

The ball is in your court to take action and write, or edit, your resume to be golden. Take this process a step at a time, and knock it out section by section.

Remember the time and effort you put into your resume and personal marketing strategy can pay itself back a thousand times over to your dream job and a better life.

The moment to act is now though! Don't waste another second.

And while you're fully equipped to write a golden resume and ace interviews, I recognize that you might want more help.

I encourage you to check out my online course MasterTheResume.com.

This program has 11 step-by-step videos to write a perfect resume and cover letter, real resume and cover letter demonstrations, and bonuses that are impossible to include in a book. This course is the exact proven system to help you stand out from the competition and get your dream job.

Check out the world-class material here:

https://mastertheresume.com

Lastly, I look forward to seeing how you traded your golden resume for a golden job. Please share your success story with me by sending a quick email to brian@takeyoursuccess.com.

Take your success,

Brian Robben

Other Work By Brian Robben

There are two different ways to manage your money and live. Most young adults use their money the wrong way. They work at jobs they don't enjoy. Buy things that don't make them happy in the long term. And are forced to work until they're 65.

Brian Robben's *Freedom Mindset* shows the other way to live. This is a step-by-step guide on how to become rich so you have the freedom to live more and work less.

Robben uncovers:

- Eight Steps To Salary Negotiation Excellence
- The most important factor to becoming rich
- How to destroy debt and stay out of debt
- Your current saving problem and what to do instead
- How to escape the rat race and retire decades early
- The truths and the lies about investing
- A winning investment strategy you can set on autopilot

If you're willing to handle your money differently than most people, this guide will put you on the fast track to get rich and reach financial freedom.

Order *Freedom Mindset* now on Amazon.com.

About The Author

Brian Robben is a serial entrepreneur and the Amazon bestselling author of three books: *How To College*, *Freedom Mindset*, and *The Golden Resume*. He also founded TakeYourSuccess.com—a top website on landing your dream job, productivity, and success that has helped thousands of readers.

Brian's work, which focuses on motivating and equipping people to reach their potential and live a successful life, has been featured on Fox News, AOL, 700 WLW, and other major publications.

He is 22 years old and currently lives in Cincinnati, Ohio.